Windows & Mirrors
Kings County Young Story Tellers

Eaglespeaker Publishing

Copyright © 2024 by The Municipality of the County of Kings

All rights reserved.

No portion of this book may be reproduced in any form without written permission from the publisher or author, except as permitted by Canadian copyright law.

Dedication

We dedicate this book to our ancestors.

We stand on the shoulders of those who came before us, as we leave room for future generations to do the same.

Table of Contents

Introduction	IX
Foreword	XI
1. Tia Sampson	1
2. Obaloluwa Mejolagbe	5
3. Deedeire Mejolagbe	9
4. Drucilla Medicraft	12
5. Daisy Stevens	16
6. Delilah Dean	22
7. Jemika Porter	26
8. Coco Coyne	33
9. Maichail Reid	42
10. Amani Mutuku	46
11. Tammy Sampson	52
Tammy Art 1.5	54
12. Santeano Barrows	56
13. Sam Akao	66
14. Mea Pleasant	70
15. Alexi-Jade Smith	74
The Publisher	77

Thank You

To our mentors we had throughout this project:

- Kathy-Ann Johnson
- Lawrence Parker
- Damini Awoyiga
- Hissa Simpson-Barrows

Introduction

Behind the Name

The name *"Windows & Mirrors"* came from a 1988 educator *Emily Style,* who believed that the act of reading gives readers the impression that they are looking through a window, watching someone else's life. The observers aren't able to relate to the experiences of a character, or given the impression that they are looking into a mirror because of how similar their experiences are to a character. Because there are not as many mainstream novels that are written by and about People of Colour, People of Colour are often left with the feeling they are looking through a window.

Windows & Mirrors is a powerful concept in literature that allows readers to either see through a window into a different world or to see themselves reflected in the characters they encounter. It is a way to bridge empathy and understanding between readers and the diverse experiences of others. By increasing representation of People of Colour in literature, we can create more mirrors for individuals to see themselves reflected and more windows for readers to gain insight into different perspectives. This project is a step towards a more inclusive and diverse literary landscape where everyone can find themselves and learn from the stories of others.

Participants engaged in a series of five workshops covering a wide range of creative mediums, including writing, poetry and visual arts where they were mentored by a diverse group of experienced authors, educators, artists, and poets. Participants were encouraged to delve into their unique voices and perspectives.

This project is funded by the *Association of Black Social Workers* (ABSW) *Youth Development Initiative* (YDI) grant and is a community partnership between the *Municipality of the County of Kings*, the *Valley African Nova Scotian Development Association* (VANSDA) and *Eaglespeaker Publishing* *(eaglespeaker.com)*.

Foreword

I remember it as clearly as an azure sky of deepest summer ... that thick dense afternoon on the *Wagmatcook* rez.

Chilling lakeside in the torrential rains, alone with seven random *rez dogs*. All eight of us are glaring Indigenously at colonization, just another day contemplating our existence and resistance – when all of a sudden, it dawns on me ... ***my existence is my resistance.***

Whoa, mind blown!

"Umm, we told you so, fight the power!" my snarky Ancestor whispers to me.

"Oh shush, you!" I whisper back.

Two shakes of lamb's tail later – I mean, literally, two nearby *rez lambs* shook their soaked tails right in my face (!) – I hear my fully-colonized non-Indigenous *iPhone* scream that de-colonized Indigenous *War Cry* I recently uploaded for my ringtone. Me and six of the rez dogs dash towards the War Cry – of course, I am the fastest.

Oh snap, a video chat??? Aww man, I totally forgot. I quickly brush my rez hair with a rez brush (aka rez tree branch), brush my rez teeth with my rez fingers, and get a stereotypically stoic rez look on my rez face.

I answer with a little bit of rez attitude, *"Who 'dis?"*

"It's Brittany, Graysen and Charissa ... and we wanna amplify kids voices!"

"*Well, you have come to the right place!*" I say confidently, desperately trying to hide the hideous moose meat stain I just noticed on my *#LandBack* hoodie.

What proceeded was a plan to take over the world ...

>Five quick weeks
>Five fantastic sessions
>Countless yummy sandwiches
>A whole buncha cool kids
>One amazing book of all books

Mere months later, I am eagerly introducing myself to eager facilitators and even eager-er kids, in Blackfoot:

"*Oki, Nis'too Niit'an'iiko O'mahk'siik'iimi Pii'tai'poyi Mok'aa'kiit I'yii'kaak'ii'maat*"

(crickets)

"*Ummmm, man, imma need a translation.*" I hear some cool kid say, representing everyone's thoughts.

"*Hello, my name is Jason Eaglespeaker. Try Hard. Be Strong.*" I say giggling.

"*Once every generation, an unborn child is chosen to be the Pii'pii'taaki (favored grandchild, basically). From birth we are given a traditional name, mine is O'mahk'siik'iimi, and we are raised traditionally by our grandparents. We are taught the immense power and responsibility of storytelling, to keep the peoples' stories and traditions and beliefs alive, generation after generation. It is an honor I accept with both pride and humility. Just as we look to our Ancestors for guidance, our Descendants will look to us for guidance - whether we like it or not (lol). What will we reveal to them? What strengths? What struggles? Our Descendants are counting on us to share our story, in our own words. 'Cause if we don't, then someone else will, and I guarantee they'll get it wrong. Today, young warriors, you embark on a new adventure – to share your stories AND become Published Authors! Over the next few weeks, you'll be learning all about writing, poetry and visual arts – from an amazing group of experienced authors, educators, artists, and poets. From there, I'm gonna compile all your powerful works into a powerful book, for the world and your Descendants to see!"*

As I pass around some samples of my past books, my keen Blackfoot warrior senses sense their young minds contemplating, articulating, formulating, deciding.

The weeks pass, the youth surpass, the submissions come in, the book comes to life, the world receives. The next generation is speaking, time for my generation to listen ...

Tia Sampson

Tia is a Grade 8 student in Kings County. While she is very quiet, the one thing that can get her talking is her love for Taylor Swift.

T – Talkative
I – Impatient
A – Annoying

Obaloluwa Mejolagbe

Obaloluwa (Oba) is a Grade 6 student in Kings County. Oba is an older brother to another participant in the program. When Oba isn't at school, he likes to spend his time playing sports!

O – Observer
B – Brilliant
A – Awesome
L – Lucky
O – Outstanding
L – Loud
U – Unique
W – Warrior
A - African

Deedeire Mejolagbe

Deedeire (Ire) is a Grade 3 student in Kings County. Before you break through Ire's shell, he is very quiet, but as soon as he gets comfortable, he enjoys playing around and having fun!

D – Dinosaur
E – English
E – Exciting
D – Determined
E – Entertaining
I – I am cool
R – Really funny
E – Energy

My Birthday

It was my birthday. I was at Boston Pizza with my sixteen friends. We all ordered chicken nuggets and french fries. I turned seven two weeks before, but a snowstorm made me have to wait.

When we put our order in, I was the last one to order. The waitress said *"I'm sorry but we are all out of chicken nuggets. You will have to wait two days before there will be enough."*

"I'll just order something else," I said and ordered a cheeseburger and fries.

We were eating, but were there for two hours before everyone finished. After that, we all left and went to my house. We played baseball because the snow was all gone. We only played for forty minutes.

At that time, we went inside and everyone sang *Happy Birthday* and we ate cake. It was an ice cream cake and it was so very good. After that, my sixteen friends went home. I went to bed.

It is finished.

Drucilla Medicraft

Drucilla is a Grade 2 student in Kings County. She has a vibrant personality and loves to play and be creative.

D – Delightful
R – Red
U – Unique
C – Caring
I – Interesting
L – Lovely
L – Loud
A – Apples

Daisy Stevens

Daisy is a Grade 3 student in Kings County. At school you can find her having fun on the monkey bars, playing with friends, or working on her math and reading. Daisy likes chatting with friends, watching TV, drawing, and playing with her sisters who are also part of the program.

Daring Adventures

Ideal

silly

yeet

Credits to ~~Glim~~ Glitch

Delilah Dean

Delilah is a Grade 5 student in Kings County. She enjoys drawing and her favourite subject at school is art. In her spare time, you can find Delilah drawing, writing, or reading. Delilah is also big sister and role model to two other participants in the program.

D – Dazzling
E – Ecstatic
L – Legendary
I – Important
L – Lovely
A – Amazing
H – Heartfelt

Delightful
extravagant
loyal
intelligent
lovely
awesome
helpful

Jemika Porter

Jemika is a Grade 10 student in Kings County. She is a proud daughter of fellow participant and best friend, Coco. Jemika enjoys playing video games and spending time with her two cats, Willow and *Rusty*. Jemika also loves moths.

J – Just a girl who loves to draw, make stories, and learn about moths. She is determined to become a comic artist.
E – Everything about comics and making stories warms her heart, she loves to draw and make stories for fun.
M – Moths are her only favourite insect, their bodies, wings, antennae, and the colours of them make them interesting.
I – In the future of her life, she is determined to become a comic artist. For her to make stories for people to enjoy.
K – Kind-hearted and curious. Always thinking up ideas for a comic.
A – A creative person at heart, loves to craft things and draw, she's a creative person.

MOTH'S

Jemika Porter

A - A wonderful creature of the night
T - The beauty of its wings shine so bright
I - In the dark it flutters, bringing delight
C - Curious eyes, looking to explore
A - Always in motion, never sitting still
S - So elegant in its movements, a true thrill
L - Little treasure to the human eye's
U - Unique in every way, they can't be subsituted
N - Named after a goddess of the moon
A - All around us, if we only take a moment to look around and appreciate

Creature

Creepy long fingers.
Red, beady eyes that glowed.
Ever-lasting horror.
Always watching.
Thin and boney, But strong.
Uncanny face proportions.
Rigid tEEth.
Everyone who see's it coming always ask: "did you see it too?"

Coco Coyne

Coco is a proud, protective single mother who goes above and beyond for her best friend and daughter, Jemika. Coco is one of the most positive people you will meet and has learned over the years that where you come from does not determine what you can do.

C – Cold outside but warm and caring inside her heart
O – Optimistic and daring look how much she's sharing
L – Loyal friend… don't worry she'll never pretend
L – Loving mamma loving sister until the end of time
E – Especially when you're in need of a friend
E – Escape the fear of not being near it's all in the clear
N – Never worry shall be your friend a sister forever amen

A - And if you're up late in the night
K – Knock on my door, and for sure you will
A – Awaken me, I'll step on the floor open the door

C – Clearing your mind and ease your pain while
O – Opening my arms embracing you with a hug
C – Clearing your fear, and wiping away your tears, yes
O – Of course long conversation over late night tea, will set us free.

My Daughter's First Day of School

On my daughter's very first day of school, she was so excited. She could barely sleep, just a little Princess. As a mother, I had a weird feeling but it's the first day of school. I get dressed to have breakfast. Everything is packed and ready for the first day.

I said, *"What do you want for dinner after your first big day of school?"*

She said, *"a Christmas ham dinner."*

Ok, let's do it. I walk to the bus stop and wait for the bus. I give her a kiss. The bus comes and takes my Pooky Bear to school ... I still have that weird feeling.

I go back home to make a Christmas ham dinner. That's what she wanted, that's what I do. At the end of the day, I go down to the bus stop and wait for the bus.

The bus comes and my daughter does not get off (?) ...

I look at the bus driver and ask if my daughter was there and he said, *"Well, I don't know."*

So, I jump up on the bus. It was parked in the middle of a busy street. I speak her name three times. Nothing. I look at the bus driver and said, *"I'm not getting off this bus until I know where my daughter is!"*

He pulls into the driveway of the apartment complex that we lived in, and I call the school on my cell phone. He's calling his boss to see if there were other children on the other bus that has a quite similar bus route. I get off the bus and I drive to the school in my car.

My daughter was on the other bus!

She made it home and is still sitting there. She's all hot and sweaty sitting on the bus. I was so happy to see her. I thank the bus driver.

We finally go home to eat our Christmas ham dinner. She had a great day at school, and she loved the school bus because it took so long to get home. The next day, she gets on the bus, and I look at the bus driver and we start laughing.

"She's coming on this bus to come home, right?" I asked.

"Yes." he said.

After school, I stand there waiting for her, she gets off the bus and she looks like she lost her best stuffie. I said *"Pookey Bear, what's a matter?"*

She said, *"I wanted to have another adventure and go for a longer bus drive"*.

To this very day, the first day of school, I take off from work. I make a full Christmas ham dinner, with all the fixings.

Making positive memories.

Love always,

First Day of School

This little girl went to her first day of school, and she was so excited!

She stands with her mother outside on a cool fall morning with the crisp mountain air. The little girl was sensitive and the wind blowing on her face took her breath away, actually making her gag a little. As the bus rolls up, her mother gives her a kiss and the little girl gets on the bus. She's in grade primary and had never been on a bus before. The other kids on the bus saw the little girl gag when she was on the side of the road and as soon as she got on the bus, they made fun of her and began teasing her mum's wild crazy hair. The little girl continued gagging as she realized that these people were talking about her.

When the little girl got off the bus, a woman took her to her class to meet her teacher. She was very shy and didn't talk much. One of the first things she remembers is the smell of the school and that pink hand soap that she washes her hands with for snack and lunch. A little girl sitting beside her in class asked if she could use her purple crayon. This was a couple days in, and she had just gotten a new pack from her teacher.

She pulled out the purple crayon and the girl said, *"thank you,"* and I, the little girl, said, *"you're very welcome."*

When the girl beside me was finished coloring, she gave back a broken crayon with the paper almost fully off it. I clearly could see her putting my new crayon in her crayon box. I asked to take her own crayon back. I was a little bit upset so I walked up and told the teacher. The teacher ended up being the mom of the other little girl who said *"Mom, she broke my crayon"*.

The mother, a.k.a. the teacher, said *"I don't care,"* and the little girl gave me back the broken crayon.

I was very upset and that has always stuck with me because the teacher didn't even pay attention to what anyone was saying. Just her daughter wanted what she wanted and wouldn't even listen to the New Girl.

Over the next few days, the school bus trip was not getting any easier. The kids on the bus were saying the little girl was stealing from their bookbags. She was not even sitting with them, as the little girl ended up sitting behind the bus driver. She used to get a lot of bloody noses because of her sensitivities - to the warm and cold – and was teased about the bloody nose.

Going back into the school, she didn't really have any friends at all. One noon hour, the kids were playing outside, and it was a cold day. The little girl got to the top of the slide and a little boy swung off the bar and pushed the little girl – she fell on the slide and hurt her lower back. The little boy was laughing when the little girl went home to her mom and told her what had happened. Her mother didn't even believe her. Even though the little girl couldn't bend down to pick up a thing, she was sore.

A few days later, she was back at school, and another little kid in the middle of the winter had jumped off the jungle gym and jumped on her. He pushed her head into the snow, and he whispered in her ear. *"We don't have (n-word)s in our school"* – he used the full N word. The little girl went home again and told her mother, who finally had to listen, not even knowing what the word meant but only that it must have been bad. My mother finally decided to move.

The little girl liked the new school much better. She made a nice friend. They would come home from school together and play. She was invited to a birthday party. Her and her friend actually both wore the exact same Michael Jackson dresses. One was a red leather dress with a white diamond glove printed on the front, the other one was a black leather dress with a white diamond glove on the dress. Not real leather (I guess we just pretend). The girls had so much fun as they danced. They enjoyed each other's company.

One day the little girl came up to her and said she had to move. The little girl had a broken heart. She still remembers her friend driving away in her father's brown Camaro, the little girl waving in the back just like in a movie. Only there was no music except for me wiping my tears away. Then I moved again. I moved three times before I ended up moving with my father, and my father was extremely strict with lots of rules. But that's a whole other story. The little girl made another friend, and we went to church together at this new school. But every friend I made ended up moving. I thought for sure God hated me.

One time when I was in Grade 6, we were in French class and the French teacher asked us to bring pictures of our home and our family. We were doing a family tree, and it was the only time in French class that we were actually allowed to speak English. I brought a picture of all my cousins. We are Black and Indigenous, a mixed race, beautiful, blended family. In the picture you can see all my cousins or at least most of them. I showed the picture around. Now it was time for questions, and I was open to any question at this point. I remember one of the guys saying, *"Wow, I always wondered why you got so dark so fast when we went outside to play at noon hour."* The rest of the class kind of laughed and giggled. But that was great, people got to know who I was or what my race was.

I always had really curly hair that I brushed every day to make it wavy. One day in Grade 8 I decided that I did not want to brush my hair and left it curly. I went to school and everyone in my grade thought I had a perm. All the girls picked on me as I told them that this was my natural curly hair. At lunch time, they made me go downstairs to the locker room, wash my hair, and let it dry to show them. Luckily for me, I didn't have any products in my hair that day, so my hair was even curlier as it dried. When the other girls saw, they stopped making fun of me and I finally started making friends.

In school, I wasn't very good at math, so I almost always stayed in at lunch time to get help from teacher. I remember one day, the teacher said to me, *"I noticed everyone you hang out with has a boyfriend or girlfriend, but you don't. If I may ask, why is that?"* and I simply said, *"Well, it took me this long to make friends. Why would I ruin it by doing that?"* He said that was a pretty damn good answer.

I ended up moving at the end of Grade 9 and lived with my mom. I went to *Horton High School*. I really loved that school. I met a lot of amazing friends, amazing people, and my first true love, who is still in my heart to this day. I got a job where I started making money for myself and doing my own things. Life was good. I moved 17 times before I got to Horton and pretty much kept to myself. Many lessons were learned in that school.

I remember working at this sandwich place. A man came in and I couldn't see his eyes, just a blue blur where his eyes were - when the man looked right at me! He said, *"You know what I kind of sandwich I want"*.

I looked up at this stranger that I had never met before and I said, *"Yes, you want a foot long whole wheat sub with crab lobster meat, with a little bit of lettuce and extra mayo, cut in half."*

The girl that was working with me looked at me and said, *"This is ridiculous"*.

Then, to my surprise, this man starts answering all these questions I've been asking my whole life: *Why do I see this? Why do I feel this? Why do I see things before it happens?* He was answering these questions, like I had already asked the questions, but I had never even seen or met him before.

Since I made him his sandwich, I was not allowed to ring it in. The other lady had to come back out and she rang in the man's meal. He placed a business card on the counter and said, *"Put your hand over this card and tell me, what do you feel?"*

The girl says *"This is ridiculous. I don't feel anything, this is so silly."*

Then I put my hand over the card, and it took my breath away. It felt like elastic rubber bands connecting the card to my hand. It's like warm and tingly. I could feel the energy. He said, *"Only special people can feel that."*

I said *"It's like energy."*

He said "Yeah, I feel that with people."

Like I said, he answered all of these questions for me. I see things that other people don't see. I feel things that other people don't. He gave me the card and went away, and I became friends with this man for many years, until his passing a few years ago. He also introduced me to a wonderful woman *Edna Ake*r, a Medium. We are like mother and daughter. I love her very much, that's another wonderful story.

When I was teenager, I tried to be the best that I could be and not allow other's opinions to affect me. I started going to the gym and became a gym junkie. I loved my life. I was by myself a lot, except for when I was at the gym or at work. I have always felt that if people don't like me, it is because they don't know me. I can't help where I come from. But I can help where I'm going. When I was a teenager, I kept really busy because I knew the type of person I didn't want to be, and what I didn't want to be like.

Growing up knowing that I was mixed race, I was never black enough ... I was never white enough. I never felt like I fit in. I spent a lot of time by myself. Even though I knew lots of people I just didn't hang out with anyone. I loved going to the dance clubs.

I am now a single, amazing, happy, thankful, grateful mother of a beautiful daughter, and the aunt of a beautiful, amazing niece. I realized that it doesn't matter what other people think about you, because when you look in that mirror you better be darn sure that you love, respect, and admire that reflection that is looking back at you. Because if you don't, you need to fix it until you do. Be the best you can be.

MAICHAIL REID

Maichail is a Grade 7 student in Kings County. He enjoys sports, especially football and basketball.

M – Magical
A – Adventurous
I – Imagining
C – Curious
H – Happy
A – A funny person
I – Ideas
L – Laughter

My Poem to Future Me

Hello Beautiful
Be better than me
Be stronger

Stand up against racism
When you're called "chocolate"
When you're called the n-word
When you hear the n-word

If you're asked where you're from
Or they assume to know
Report anything that is wrong
Or feels wrong

Do the right thing
You know, when you get the 'Stamp of Approval'
It may come from someone bigger than you
But it doesn't have to, it can come from someone younger

Believe in yourself and know you can always do it.

Amani Mutuku

Amani is a Grade 6 student in Kings County. Before making her way to Nova Scotia, her and her family spent time living in Australia. Amani is active in her middle school band where she plays the clarinet.

A – Amazing
M – Majestic
A – Astounding
N – Nice
I – Independent

Will Dad Be Okay?

It was a beautiful sunny day in Sydney, Australia. I was at Bankstown central with my mom. It was a girl's day out.

"Isn't it a nice day to go to the mall, Iris?" said Mom.

"Yeah, what are we going to buy, Mom?" I said, "Remember two new outfits, new school supplies, a new bag, and a water bottle, finally three new pairs of shoes".

It was the first day of school, and my best friend Sarah was in my class again! For three years in a row, we almost got separated because we couldn't stop talking to each other because that's when my parents bought me my first phone, but it was an emergency, right? Anyway, back on topic....

Michelle was in my class again – ugh! She bullied me for years.

"*Hey punk!*" Michelle said. I ignored her and kept walking.

"*Look like you finally changed your look.*" she said.

Snickers echoed down the hallway where my sister Ember was talking to her friends. Ember stopped talking to her friends, stomped all the way over, got up in Michelle's face and hollered *"STOP BULLYING MY SISTER, or else!"*

Michelle took off crying in the girl's bathroom. I bet she peed her pants. Sometimes Em has that effect on people. *"Thanks for the save Ember."*

"No problem, but you really need to learn how to defend yourself, Iris. Otherwise it's going to be tough in middle school," said Ember.

"I'll keep working on it."

"Well, that was dramatic," said Sarah. *"Talk about dramatic! What class are you in?"*

"Six Lorade."

Most of the day was uneventful except for the teacher telling me to pay attention.

"BEEEEEP!"

Every student starts packing up their books, then Mrs. Warner tells us to stop digging so we can listen to the announcements. It goes something like this ... "*and we have a winter social this Thursday, today is Tuesday, remember there's band till 3:30-4:15, boys and girls cross country swimming tryouts is happening tomorrow at first lunch in the pool room.*"

Me and Sarah's eyes pop open when we hear that! The pool room is only used for special occasions!!

When me and Sara walk home, we talk about the cross-country swimming tryouts, *"Do you wanna tryout for the cross-country swim club?"*

"Well, I don't know if I can join because I might have dance...."

"Well, that's okay if you don't want to join because we have to check out schedules first." I said.

"Want to come over to my house?"

"Sure, I just need to tell my mom."

Once my house popped into view my dad was mowing the lawn. *"Hi girls!"*

"Hi Mr. Brown," dad's smile looked forced.

Once we got inside my bedroom, Sarah said, *"your dad is acting really weird…."*

"Well maybe he's having a bad day?"

Then suddenly we heard these coughing and hacking noises outside on the front lawn … will Dad be okay?

Tammy Sampson

Tammy is an active community member of the local African Nova Scotian community. She values bringing folks together. Tammy keeps busy attending different community events, taking part in committees, and constantly adding more responsibilities to her to-do list.

T – Terrific
A – Amazing
M – Majestic
M – Magnificent
Y – Youthful

Y — Youthful
T — Terrific
M — Magnificent
M — Majestic
A — Amazing

Santeano Barrows

Santeano is a Grade 6 student in Kings County. Santeano is very outgoing and steps up to be a leader among her peers. You can also find Santeano on the soccer field.

S – Smart
A – Athlete
N – Nature
T – Talented
E – Entertaining
A – Awesome
N – Noteworthy
O – Original

Star

A star is what you are
Amongst them is where you belong

With them you will stand
How you get to them is up to you

So don't shortchange yourself
You are a star and that is very true

So remember if you shoot for the moon
and miss at least you will land in the stars
What are you waiting for
It is your time to shine

The World

The world is yours to enjoy
For you to explore
Do you think you can conquer?
Think of all the places
You can indulge in
Things you can experience
New terrains to traverse
And new cultures to explore

When I close my eyes I can feel the coarseness of Kuwait's sandy deserts
The heat and shine of Jamaica and some of America's sun
The cold and darkness of Canada's winters

There are 195 countries of the world
It has always been my dream to visit all of them
It may be yours too

Do you think you can rise to the occasion?
I do
Remember, the world is yours

The Horror Ship

It was the year 3000. A spaceship was launched and the people cheered, but little did they know that it would turn sour.

Astronaut Ed White was doing a routine check on the outside of the ship. Then, just as he gave the all clear, the oxygen tank in his space suit cracked. Oxygen mixed with the fuel in his jetpack and created an explosion.

Chapter One: In Space No One Can Hear You Scream

Insert Astronaut James Cann. It was 12 o'clock when James heard a crash, so he went to investigate it. When he got to the source of the sound nothing was there, except a broken cup. He turned around and a slimy black monster opened the airlock. James went flying into space. He tried to scream, but it was no use, no one could hear him.

So he just sat there in space waiting for his lungs to explode, when something ruptured inside him.

Chapter Two: The News

It started like any normal day for the astronauts' families, until 7 pm when the news started. As they watched - BREAKING NEWS: two astronauts dead, James Cann and Ed White – the families were in shock and disbelief. Reporters said GASA (Global Aeronautics and Space Association) is sending two astronauts to replace them, Elsa Twetie and Amani Mantuko. The rocket is to be launched on Saturday.

Chapter Three: The Explosion

It was early Saturday morning and the Stargazer Rocket was launching soon, so the technicians calculated how much fuel it would need.

Guy number one *"so, if you were to go to the space station which is 3,200 km above the Earth's surface we would need approximately 4,000 gallons of fuel in each stage."*

Guy number two said *"no, you would need 10,000 because if it's 3,200 miles away we would need 10,000 Gallons of fuel if we want to make a round trip."*

So, they fueled the ship with 10,000 gallons of fuel *"Better to be safe than sorry."*

But in this case they would be sorry.

The launch is now in final preparations. Technician Zayne Corkcum is on his lunch break when someone yells *"Hey fix that bolt!"*

"OK," Zayne replied, then went over quickly and screwed in the bolt so he could get back to his lunch. Little did he know that his incompetence would lead to disaster.

"T-minus 10 seconds till liftoff, 9 seconds, 8 seconds, Ignition sequence starts, 5 Seconds, 4 seconds, 3 seconds, 2 seconds, 1 second, blast off." says the announcer over the P.A. system.

"So far so good," yelled Elsa.

"Yeah," said Amani

Then **KABOOM**, the sky lit up like 1,000 suns as the astronauts were vaporized in an instant - the heat was felt one mile below! Everyone ran in a different directions to avoid the burning shrapnel. Underwater was no different. The blast created a tidal wave so massive the bedrock underneath was pulverized and fish were cooked alive. Divers' organs ruptured and a massive tsunami was now on course to hit Denver.

Chapter Four: The Discussion

Back on the spaceship a meeting has been called.

"We need to address the truth here, we need to do something about these deaths!" said one astronaut.

"Hey watch your tone man I am the captain I make the decisions around here!!" said Captain Mason.

"He's out of line, but he's right. Here take these weapons and go fight the monster if you're so confident private," Lieutenant Gunhee told the astronaut.

"But what if I die," the astronaut asked.

"No buts, you are doing it anyway," said Captain Mason.

"Just give him someone to go with," Lieutenant Gunhee pleaded.

"Fine", said Captain Mason, *"Sergeant Zeke get your butt over here!"*

"Whaddya want?" asked Sergeant Zeke.

"I need you to go with that private", said Captain Mason.

"Fine", said sergeant Zeke.

Chapter Five: The Hunter Becomes The Hunted

"*I repeat this is Sergeant Zeke, I am being chased by the monster. The other astronaut with me was killed in action. I am low on ammo. The monster is right behind me AHHHHHHHHHH - that was his last entry*" said Captain Mason over intercom to Sergeant Zeke's family.

"*We still haven't found him*", he said in a sorrow voice, "*We think he is K.I.A*"

Zeke's little sister Lucy sobbed "*He was such a good big brother*".

On the opposite end of the spectrum.

"*Lets gooooooooo!*" the rest of Zeke's family screamed, "*Now we can use the computer more!*"

"*Now I can take all his money*", Lucy exclaimed.

So, they took all Zeke's money and they divvied it up. They each got three million. Then they split up his shares in the stock market and each earned ten million more. They were now rich out of their minds, but it would not last long.

Chapter Six: The Investigation

One day on the spaceship - "*Sir, our cameras spotted something last night take a look*", said a random tech guy.

Captain Mason walked over and took a look at the footage. He saw a black slimy monster with one eye rise up out of the ground and there were eyes everywhere. Then he saw an astronaut run from it. He got far, but the black slimy hands got him.

Captain Mason shuddered "*ugh, but I must investigate*".

So he took the keys and went through door number one. Then he went through door number two. Then 20 more doors. Then he got rushed and he died.

"*Welp looks like I'm in charge,*" said the acting Captain, Gunhee.

Suddenly he heard a dreaded sound *"Oh no, the reactor is melting, everyone into the escape pod!!!"* Gunhee yelled.

So they all piled up in an escape pod and blasted off, but before they could leave the blast radius the nuclear explosion incinerated them.

Oh nooo!

                Inspired by: Saving Private Ryan, Marvel movies, Among Us (videogame)

Sam Akao

Sam Akao is a grade 6 student in Kings County. Sam enjoys hanging out and watching TV, but you can also find on the soccer field and squash courts!

S – Super
A – Amazing
M – Marvelous

I Don't Know What to Write

I don't know what to write
Am I going crazy I don't know
Maybe I am but hopefully not

Basically I'm very bored
Other than writing this poem I really have nothing to do
Exactly what should I do

Do I though, on this long day

Mea Pleasant

Mea is a Grade 4 student in Kings County. She enjoys spending time playing on her iPad, drawing, and listening to Taylor Swift. You can also find Mea swimming competitively, playing basketball or playing soccer!

Alexi-Jade Smith

Alexi-Jade is a Grade 6 student in Kings County where she takes part in band. Alexi is enjoys writing, being social and spending time with her friends.

A – Awesome
L – Leader
E - Eloquent
X – X-factor
I – Impactful

My Beautiful Skin

My skin is black and beautiful. Its the skin I walk in, talk in, and rock in.

It's the skin that makes me confident, unique and the skin that makes me special. When I do my hair and wear nice clothes I shine, just like a star in the midnight sky. When all the colors of the rainbow are combined, that shade is as beautiful as mine.

My hair is the texture of lamb's wool, soft thick rich and curly.
My skin is black and beautiful. It's the same color as the rich dark soil.

That harvests the food we need.
My black skin shows power and strength.

My skin! My hair! What a blessing it is.
I smile and dance cause its what I've got.
My skin! My hair! A curse it's not.

The Publisher

O'MAHK'SIIK'IIMI (aka Jason EagleSpeaker)

Only a few short years after the ***Occupation of Alcatraz***, *the* ***Wounded Knee Incident*** and the ***Shootout at Pine Ridge Reservation****,* a boy was conceived.

Born in Seattle, raised on four reservations and in two cities, Jason EagleSpeaker is both Blackfoot (mom) and Duwamish (dad). He is an award winning internationally published Author, Illustrator and Publisher of over 350 books (with Authors from over 275 First Nations). His hard hitting true stories focus on revealing Indigenous peoples' modern experiences.

You can easily connect with Jason online through social media (Facebook, LinkedIn) or via his website - eaglespeaker.com

NAPI CHILDREN'S BOOKS:

- Napi and the Rock
- Napi and the Bullberries
- Napi and the Wolves
- Napi and the Buffalo
- Napi and the Chickadees
- Napi and the Coyote
- Napi and the Elk
- Napi and the Gophers
- Napi and the Mice
- Napi: The Anthology

GRAPHIC NOVELS:

- UNeducation: A Residential School Graphic Novel
- Napi the Trixster: A Blackfoot Graphic Novel
- UNeducation, Vol 2: The Side of Society You Don't See On TV

LEARN SOME BLACKFOOT:

- My First Blackfoot Word Book
- My First Blackfoot Word Coloring Book

COLLABORATIONS:

- Young Water Protectors
- Young Native Activist
- Sober Indianz
- Indigenous Peoples for BlackLivesMatter
- I Am The Opioid Crisis
- The Great Cheyenne
- The Empowerment of Eahwahewi
- Descendants of Warriors
- Hello … Fruit Basket
- How The Earth Was Created
- I Am The Opioid Crisis
- My Ribbon Skirts
- My Kokum Scarves
- Crow Brings Daylight
- Spite No.1 and No.2
- Aahksoyo'p Nootski Cookbook
- Four Directions Thunderbird Woman
- … and many many more at **eaglespeaker.com**

If you loved this book, be sure to find it online and leave a quick review. Your words help more than you realize.

Also, be sure to check out plenty more authentically Indigenous publications at eaglespeaker.com

Manufactured by Amazon.ca
Bolton, ON

38323303R00059